The Heart Hungers for Wildness

The Heart Hungers for Wildness

poems by

Diane Glass

Zion Publishing

Cover Art: Tall Trees/Loess Hills by Concetta Morales.

Back cover photograph by Brent Isenberger at Brent Isenberger Photography, Des Moines, Iowa.

Photo taken from the author's personal connection.

Epigraph is from a lecture titled, "Walking," by Henry David Thoreau delivered several times beginning in 1851.

ISBN: 978-1-7357958-4-3

The Heart Hungers for Wildness is available online or in bulk orders from the author at: Dianeglass96@gmail.com

Zion Publishing
Des Moines, Iowa
www.zionpublishing.org

To Jeff

Eileen and Sue

All good things are wild and free
Henry David Thoreau

Contents

Hunger

Heart

Wildness

Hunger

Soup Saves the World

I have magic powers: my chicken soup
cures colds, the flu, brings down fevers,
launches sick children and adults out of bed.

Problems with digestion? Try my bean soup.
Swim with carrots and kale to improve your gut,
brighten your skin, firm up your bones.

Mourn your lost love? Shed genuine tears
while chopping onions for Ribollita.

Feeling weak? Hustle a jicama, subdue a squash,
smash a garlic head to release your inner aria.

Savor the curves of a red bell pepper,
the heady aromas of basil and thyme.
Listen to sultry jazz to flaunt your culinary skills.

Bring together fast food refugees
for bowls of your brew. Care for Mother Earth:
use just enough meat to make a good broth.

Learn from the world's cooks how cumin's
smokiness saturates India, paprika's sweet pepper
grounds Hungarian goulash, ginger root's kick warms
up China, lemons mimic the Mediterranean sun
to light up Turkish taste buds.

Prepare your favorite bisque, gumbo or chowder,
invite over friends, uncork a bottle of wine.
Open the door to a world transformed.

Sturdy Table Legs

I watched her eyeball the wood beads
encircling my oak top. She studied my legs—
carved wooden globes and etched rectangles.
Perfect for my condo, she said.

Before long, I hosted supper: soup and salad,
freshly baked scones, catching up on
the day's news, friends, and sisters.

Then bill-paying, Canasta, vacation planning,
family dinners with platters of sweet corn,
lasagna and cherry pie. Children chatter
underneath me, their castle.

People grieve on me, heads in hands,
reading cancer lab reports, mourning
a son's death, planning a funeral.
Casseroles, cards and flowers collect on me.

A son proposes to a woman from India.
Articles on arranged marriage, packing tips
and airline schedules to Delhi clutter my surface.

Lemon oil buffs my red oak to a shine.
Great-grandma's rose Haviland china and
Waterford crystal candle holders dress me up.

One day, someone new will take me home,
add a new leaf, refinish my wood,
and make me their own.

Piecing Together a Life

I was afraid as I sat in a warm pool of light,
sewing my clothes for school. Magically,
collar came to neck, Bodice A to Bodice B,
side zippers to skirts and pants.

Adhering to instructions, I transformed
pink flowered cotton into sundresses,
wide wale corduroy to jackets, black and white
percale to blouses, red plaid wool to pleated skirts.
The old Singer hummed, whirred in my attic retreat.

Below, Dad clinked supper dishes in soapy water,
the black and white television laughed
1960's family sitcoms, Susie chatted on the phone.
The window overlooking main street,
devoid of cars and people, spoke of emptiness.

If I kept my eyes on seams, hems and buttonholes,
I avoided the dark space behind flimsy wood doors,
paint peeling, in the storage area to my left.
At age five, I discovered treasures there:
an Indian chief head, an old wooden trunk filled
with lace and velvet, a Charlie McCarthy doll.

But years later, sounds of family were out of reach.
Nimble fingers tensed. Eyes drifted from bringing
thread to cloth. The downpour of light from above
no longer protected me from anticipated darkness,
the unexpected, the difficult, the tragic
and so much to come:

A predatory boss in my first job, a failed marriage,
my stepson's taking his life, breast cancer.
Aging deepened my desire to make all the pieces fit.
Joy erupted too, a new romance, a second marriage.

Chaos brings integration, but until then,
instructions nag with irrelevance, seams unravel,
tools rust in closets. Random ribbons from bolts
of silks laced with gold, swatches of old blue
flannel shirts, quilted squares of red and green,
burlap resistant to shape—all assert their place
in a life not envisioned yet real.

Worn, flawed, flexible, curious, even beautiful,
I now become myself.

Inspired by May Sarton's poem, "Now I Become Myself."

The Ultimate Lie

I advertised myself in the classifieds,
yes, my body, my charm, my worldliness.
The ad tested this *Datemaker* thing.
Is it legit, matching reasonably sane souls?
Or does it introduce lonely women to axe murderers?
(Mind you, I was not looking for myself.)

My ad sounded ordinary enough:
      Loves Life. Single woman, 44,
      looking for kind, intelligent man
      with a good sense of humor
      who enjoys travel, cooking and music.

I avoided clichés like "loves long walks in the country."
Why walk in the country with an axe murderer?
City parks near police stations are a better choice.

So it was not my fault I actually met a nice man,
a kind, intelligent man, who said he responded
only to make sure this *Datemaker* was the real deal
before recommending it to clients.
He's a therapist, you see.

It was not his fault he liked me and I liked him.
We hung out for a few years, bought a house,
got married, and to this day defend the ultimate lie:
Neither of us was lonely.

Life on Remote

The pandemic deprives me
of coloring my grey hair, wearing
my new slinky black dress, savoring
stellar symphony sounds and deft moves
from dance troupes in the Civic Center.

Our trip to the big island of Hawaii,
a 25th wedding anniversary, postponed.
Cook-at-home concoctions replace
restaurant-plated dinners with decorative aioli.
The grandchildren and I practice their piano
virtually without the joy of a hug.

Many live life on remote without relief—
the man with spina bifida who collects
superhero figures for company,
the elderly woman who watches daytime TV
to hear human voices in her silent house.
The young man with schizophrenia
shunned by apartment neighbors
and the undocumented immigrant
pushed to the shadows by officials
know isolation beyond the pandemic.

For now, my husband and I dance
a cheek-to-cheek two-step
on the vinyl kitchen floor,
our new grand ballroom.

The Other Side of the Wall

A homeless man died last week
on the outside of the east wall
of our church where I offer
prayers of healing on Sunday.

I was inside, near the grand piano,
under stained glass windows,
sheltered by the stucco archway.

> *I lay my hands upon you*
> *in the name of our Savior Jesus Christ,*

He slept on the cement near
an exhaust fan offering scant warmth.
We invited him to Wednesday's
free supper. He declined.

Did we hear his final breaths
or did we smother them with hymns?
Did we do enough to save him?
Do I do enough?

> *praying that he will uphold you,*

The pastor noted the event
in a line item in the bulletin,
"homeless man, name unknown,"
with names of other church members
who had died, are sick or grieving.
Let's pray for him today, she said.

> *and fill you with grace*

On Epiphany Sunday we recognize
the divinity of the Baby Jesus,
as the Magi did, following
the Star of Bethlehem.

We too are called to see
the presence of God in everyone,
including the homeless.

Did the wall between us
blind my vision, my insight?

> *that you will know the healing*
> *power of God's love.*

The century-old almond-hue stucco
stands strong. Windows cast fragments
of blue and green. When I offer God's blessing
of comfort and reassurance, my heart cries out,
a love letter never received, never sent.

Feast

God suffocated my senses
as a passing priest flung
Sweet Byzantine Rose incense
from a brass censer.

Humid August air pressed in from
windows cranked open.

God generated heat and fragrance,
the taste of paper communion hosts
stuck to the roof of my mouth,

the sound of come-to-the-kingdom
hymns, and the touch of blessing oil
on my forehead. The vision of
a crucified Christ on a cross.

In my child's mind, Purgatory lurked
behind the vents flanking the altar,
emitting heat, imprisoning poor souls
paying for earthly sins.

Jesus, that big brother
with brown hair and blue eyes,
assuaged my fear with gentle arms
and stories of welcoming multitudes
with baskets of fish and bread.

Today, I feast on flesh and bone,
imbibe wine, and inhale scents
of rosemary and anise
with family and friends.
Is God not here?

The Call

Sister Elizabeth's black habit and rosary beads
brush the back of my head.

You may have a call from God to be a nun, she says.

I pray the rosary and recite indulgences
to reduce purgatory time. Yet becoming a nun
means replacing plaid skirts with heavy robes,
lacy collars with stiff headdresses,
boys with marriage to the Lord.

Can I still get to heaven if I don't become a nun?
I choke on my brave words.

Maybe, but at a lower rung. She floats by.

Clinging to my purple Baltimore catechism,
I pray to God for a sign: a burning bush,
an angel descending, a loud command.

Dreams of traveling stone corridors to Mass
at dawn in a novice robe too thin for this
unheated monastery interrupt my sleep.

I wake to hear birds at dawn, not church bells
or a priest's admonition, only God's invitation
to play, and my dad's gentle reminder
that the oatmeal is waiting.

The Piano Speaks

Always you come back to what you found
in childhood. Or did it find you?

On dreamy days, we play Chopin or Brahms,
imagining a stone portico, green fronds
softening the edges, a beautiful lady in periwinkle
playing a Prelude or Intermezzo, silencing birds.

Precise days, Bach presides amid marble and gold:
the erotic persistence of a Partita, the dance of a
Sarabande, austerity of a fugue, or grandeur of a
concerto before suited gentlemen, corseted ladies
in gowns with appropriate applause.

You and your mother rushed through Russian duets,
a competition to reach the end, a decision to play
the coda or not, laughter erupting as notes
fell victim to inaccuracy. Applause for speed.

Is that why rhythm eludes you? Pound out
the beats with your metronome. I'm being
too harsh. Few reach Rubinstein or de Larrocha.

We're silent for weeks, no months. Where is
my music, my art? Where are you?
My keys are here, the hammers, strings, soundboard.
When will you bring me to life?

Sanctuary

The remote practice room is mine, a back porch
with windows, panes mottled, fractured light falling
upon the old upright piano, worn elegance.

Nuns once lived in this house, sitting on this porch
in light summer robes, watching possums dart
across the green lawn under old weeping willows.

Did they sit tall like the piano I am about to play,
hands folded or holding black leather Bibles,
or did they slump and sleep in rocking chairs,
free from prayer and duty?

The Bach Italian Concerto fits this place: stately,
somber, sad. I strike the notes, startled by the clarity
and pitch of an old Steinway that holds its integrity.

Who listens to my playing? The rain hitting the panes,
the possums, the willow, the walls of this place
that know prayer?

Who hears the silence between the notes?

Talking to Pain

I remember the very summer morning
when wind ballooned ivory lace curtains
into ladies' wedding gowns. Sunshine
coated my cat snoring on a fuzzy rug.
I lay in bed, each muscle luxuriating.
My sacrum fractured the next day.

The weeks after breast cancer treatment
I was light with joy, fear drained away.
These days were a gift to a new future.
I sipped white wine in a crystal glass,
packed my peach cashmere sweater
for a celebratory trip to the city.
In a suite overlooking a jeweled skyline,
my legs began to shake uncontrollably,
beginning a lifetime with restless legs.

Fire burns my toes, spasms stab my heels,
my feet cry to get out of bed, trusting
my attention will shift to morning coffee,
the newspaper, breakfast with Jeff.

I accept you're here to stay.
What can I learn from you?
How can I not become you?

We rest in the predawn, sharing
the recliner, a frequent retreat.
Our long history brings the comfort
of familiarity, of intimacy,
if not pleasure or relief.

Resurrection

On the sunny college campus, students walk
to stately structures, talking poets, parties,
postgrad studies, focused on life, not death.

Marble steps show shallow dips, footsteps
to library archives. Dust motes float in filtered sun,
descend on oak tables worn smooth.

I pull heavy journals from shelves, stiff board covers
nicked with age, releasing dust, neglect,
secrets, not opened for decades:

*The Journal for Developmental Medicine and
Neurology* (1956-1962): One in 25 babies
with severe spina bifida not treated at birth
survived after two years.

In time doctors drain fluid from baby's brains.
But not 1947. *Take her home to die,*
Mother remembers. A ghostly glimmer

of lost lives, dead for decades, chills the air,
the sun shifts, the room darkens.
The clock nears five. I pack up the past.

Sounds of students draw me to this summer day.
Shadow and sun intermingle, past and present
come together, sadness companions joy.
History yields insight, not answers.

The soul asks, free of certainty, wise to the heart,
How do you want to live?

Curiosity

A yellow butterfly
peers in my window
three feet away,
light shining through
wisps of wings.

Seconds before, it flitted
through lush summer leaves
of oak trees, random revelry.

It hovers. I hold my breath.

I Blame the Train Whistle

in the still humid August night
of our small Iowa town,
imagining Parisians going to Moscow,
not grain to river barges.

Or *Time* magazine's insistence
on publishing mesmerizing maps,
of Marrakech and Casablanca,
Tunisian deserts and the Ganges River,
saved for my scrapbook.

Childhood primed by trips to big cities
to see *Finian's Rainbow, The King and I,*
and *Brigadoon*—on the evening
a Scottish Highlands village emerged
moments after the rain stopped.

Orient Express films: beautiful women
in slanted felt hats with feathers
on trains across Siberia
who tracked down murderers
of elderly women wearing
pearls and Pomeranians.

Travel scuffs my journal—
Tunis to sniff out saffron and anise,
Japanese ryokans for sober-faced weddings,
the Baltic Sea for Akvavit-fueled ship adventures,
Rome to walk the Coliseum, yearning
for the ghostly rumbling of trains.

The Heart Hungers for Wildness

The dirt-moving equipment beeps
as it backs up outside my window.
Not far from our condo with its ordered
gardens and fenced-in grass,
the Iowa prairie calls me to play.

My heart hungers for this wildness,
for rivers that tumble over rocks
to unknown destinations downstream,
prairies that blaze, releasing
seeds dormant for decades,
strikes of lightning and clashes
of thunder in the night.

Escaping the confines of the city,
I go there, imagining this piece of prairie
defies soybean fields and shopping malls
to reclaim the plains, rolling hills
and grasslands now subdued.

Dozens of dragonflies dive overhead,
flashing iridescence at the sun. Thorny
orbs of a rattlesnake master plant
spring through the swaying big bluestem.
Baby bison and elk, hidden from view,
rout through fields near their mothers.

Spiny barbs of native grass
prickle the soles of my feet.
Warm dirt restores me.

Heart

Pockets Full of Stories

Tell us a story, my grandchildren say.

Soma and Raadhya have an Indian mother
and an American father, my stepson,
matched in marriage by a swami.
They mesh Hindi with English,
curries with pizza, Hanuman and Jesus,
khaki shorts and kurta pajamas,
swamis and Santa Claus.

*Your mama was brave to leave behind
her family and her small Himalayan village
to start a new life with your papa,* I say.
*Like her, my grandmother crossed
an ocean to join my grandfather.*

Twirling the globe, I continue the story.

I. Leaving for America

Vera Popchuck, 1885-1962
Born: Antoniny, Russia
Died: Cedar Rapids, Iowa.

Her dilemma: what to bring, what to leave—
a heather shawl woven with wildflowers and straw,
a comfort on wintry nights by wood stoves, low fuel.

Scuffed leather shoes, smooth soles, burnished
by soil, a brown woolen coat, inside pockets full
of old stories, worn, mostly true, hope and tragedy.

A wrinkled map with plot lines, the young hands that
tended the garden now cracked with fault lines,
memories, children lost to hunger, war all around.

Photos of ten siblings, five now dead from disease,
of a deceased mother and father who worked
harvesting crops while she raised the family.

A linen blouse, cross-stitched for dancing,
a gilded flowered cup, a woven fan to ease heat,
a wedding ring sewn in a pillow.

At each hand, a child with a note pinned to her coat:
name, destination, where she belonged,
in English, not Ukrainian.

Poverty and war brought my grandfather here,
not her: a homemaker and gardener, yearning
for peace, free of fear of losing their home.

On the last ship to cross before WWI, arriving
at Ellis Island, she must have wondered,
Will the Old World matter to the New?

II. The American Dream

A bed in every room, a stove with an oven:
this rented house sheltered my grandparents
and the family that would grow to six.

My grandmother opened the door to others,
Russian immigrants like themselves
needing a place to begin their new life.

My grandfather, a skilled shoe repairman,
opened a shop for people who made
old shoes last, rather than buying new.

Grandmother saved the money she made
by providing room and board to new arrivals
to America, like herself and my grandfather,
in a jar behind the beans, flour and beets.
One day she surprised my grandfather
with enough to buy a home of their own.

Along the way, she taught herself to read
and speak English. She never went to school,
yet sent her children to college.

This is what we mean by the American Dream,
I say to my grandchildren, the opportunity
to build a life from the ground up.

I Come from the Stillness of a Small Town

We had one main street, an undertaker,
a café, a grocery store, a school, and
a stretch of asphalt for roller skating.

Frog choruses chirped in water-filled ditches,
the occasional car revved its motor,
and my sewing machine hummed
as I made jumpers and skirts.

Summers, I burrowed through the small library,
finishing a book each day, savoring
the sound of turning pages.

At supper, sparse with talk, we slurped soup,
washed dishes in soapy water, and retreated
to our rooms to read or play board games.

Silence took root in my soul, creating space
for wandering, for gazing at corn stalk oceans,
for lying under maple tree canopies,
for playing solitaire on a child's card table.

With time, this sanctuary gave way
to ringing telephones, rancorous opinions,
rumbling newspaper presses, customer complaints.
My heart withered.

Skywalks connecting concrete buildings obscured
the blue sky, home to my dreams. Illness arrived
to reveal my inner garden's need for tending.

I have returned to the quiet, my job now
to listen. What wants to be said, what the ear
of the heart hears, what the dragonfly,
the frog, and the wind have to say.

Swept Away

I slip away from the bungalow
where Mother sleeps and sister Susie
watches "I Love Lucy" in shorty pajamas,
remains of Dad's oatmeal stack in the sink,
and the next Nancy Drew mystery beckons.

Sleeves wait to be eased in armholes,
abandoned limbs on the sewing machine.
Our black party-line phone has nothing to say.

Mourning doves coo, dragonflies soar
over coreopsis, dahlias, marigolds.
I pull out my girls' Schwinn bike
and head out of town,

where barely a mile away, I greet my gravel road,
and corn, ripe with tassels ready to be pulled
by crews of teens, wave a welcome,
grasshoppers fling their bodies with exuberance.

Barn swallows with dusty blue feathers
and orange throats soar overhead,
scooping up gnats and mosquitoes.
Cars stir up dust. I cover my face.
Drivers tip their hats or raise
a single finger, the farmer salute.

The silence, the solitude, remind me
who I am beyond ten years old, shy,
studious, the brain as I am known.
I don't have to be anything here
except swept away by the beauty
of aloneness in a July Iowa summer.

Just Another White Person

I grew up unaware
of my blessings,
able to stroll across
an open field to school
or down the street
to Mrs. Wilson's
for piano lessons.

One Black family lived
on a nearby farm.
The kids came to school.
I never saw their parents.
We never thought of
ourselves as racist.

We drove to the Rocky Mountains
for vacation, our car windows
rolled down for air, and stayed
in Best Westerns along the way.

We roller-skated on main street,
asking the furniture dealer
to start up his popcorn machine,
the librarian to show us new books.
My aunt loaned me money
for college tuition.

Now we buy computers for
our grandchildren,
pay for their piano lessons,
contribute to their college fund.

I am a white-person—blind
to my privilege. Am I just passing it on,
or paying it forward?

George Floyd

He chilled our hearts
with his face, cavalier,
his knee on your neck,
George Floyd, yet another
Black man caught up in
escalation of the moment.

Mama, you cried.

We cried for you
and the thousands
of Black people killed
by police before you,
2,018* since 2013.

Yet I struggle to remember
their names:

> *Tamir Rice*
> *Freddie Gray*
> *Eric Garner*
> *Michael Brown*

My memory stops short.
Will I remember you?

*Vox and CBS News

Remembering Lonnie Dixon

He's a remote presence off to the edge
of my memory, of my life. The only Black kid
in my class. I said hi to him but not much more.

His face was missing from class photos.
Was he ill on picture day? He disappeared
after school. Where did he go? Years later,
I heard he worked on his family's tenant farm.

Not one to raise his hand in class or join
in kick-the-can games, he waited
for an invitation that rarely came, a kid
on the sidelines with a tentative smile.

Is he alive? I search for his obituary.

Lonnie Dixon, 50, died of cancer in Los Angeles
where he worked on an oil rig. He is buried
in his parents' cemetery plot in Iowa.

I wish I had been braver:
What do you do after school?
Want to be on the Homecoming committee?
How does it feel to be the only Black student?

Jerry Perkins's Mom

Jerry Perkins's mom peered into my face,
sheers in hand, pausing from pruning the roses
in the Art Center garden. *Are you okay?*
She scrunched her face.

I stopped my routine, swinging my upper body
like a pendulum, right to left, left to right.
I kept my eye on her cutting shears.
I'm okay, I really am, I told her.

Each morning before sunrise, my ritual began
in the dark, continuing until the emerging light
dispersed the potent chi. That this was
Jerry Perkins's mom was a complete surprise

until Jerry Perkins arrived one day to check out
my weird, puzzling behavior, not only the pendulum
swinging, but the wailing and gesturing.

Jerry observed from a distance, even though
we once worked together at the newspaper.
He and his mom talked quietly.

An old Chinese Qigong master taught me
this ritual of wailing and swinging in the wilderness
of Montana just days after I found out about
his retreat for cancer patients.

You right. You wrong. He circulated among us
to determine whether our tonals, as he called them,
were strong. *You right,* he said to me,
as he listened to my HAAA!, buoying my confidence
in using HAAA! to destroy cancer cells
and boost my immune system.

Now I needed the approval of Jerry Perkins's mom
who knew something after all about trimming away
disease and death, opening bushes to health.

My son Jerry tells me you're meditating,
she said, sheers nowhere in sight. *You just howl
all you want.* We went back to work.

My cancer receded by fall, the roses bloomed
with potent energy, their color and lushness
drawing people to the garden.

Who did the healing that summer?
What made the roses bloom?

Praise to the Feet

Praise to the feet that danced the polka
with boys in the Oelwein Armory,
feet that flew off the floor, so strong, so sure.
Hop, step, step, hop, step, step.

Praise to the feet that studied the Schottische
in Chicago neighborhood gyms with locals,
spirits soaring, checkered skirts swirling,
one two three hop, step hop, step hop.

Praise to the feet that tackled the tango
in adult education with agreeable boyfriends,
sultry sauntering, flinging, advancing, retreating,
step step close, step step close.

Praise to the feet that married a graceful man
who danced as a boy, thanks to his mom,
who waltzes with skill, circle right, circle left,
one two three, one two three.

Praise to the feet that danced with children
to Hindi music frenzy with energy
on carpeted living rooms on snowy days,
step rock rock, run, jump, hop, circle round, rock.

Praise to the feet that first felt pain,
arches clenched in spasms, released only by ice,
feet that still danced, hoping for relief,
step, step, pause, stop, step, step, pause, stop.

Praise to the feet that rested for weeks
and months, sturdier shoes remembering
leather soles gliding across wood floors.

Praise to the feet that grieved, crumpled in balls,
reliving Rumba's riveting rhythm,
step, step, close, step, step, close.

Praise to the feet that surrendered to the slow
shuffle, arms entwined, cheek to cheek,
close enough to whisper,
I love you, step, rock, step, rock.

Praise to the feet that walk on the earth,
meadowlark music, dirt roads,
sauntering soles, a cane my companion,
step step step, wonder, step step, step, joy.

People in the Tree

Do you see people in that tree?
My downstairs neighbor asks about Queen Maple,
majestic, wise with age, what a tree should be.
I want to see what she sees, a party going on
in the branches, leaves quivering with excitement.
It's only at night, she says.

When darkness drapes color over branches,
I stare at the tree from our porch, looking
for folks telling jokes, tidbits of gossip
about those who live around here.

Dismissing squirrels and bird nests, peering
for arms, legs, torsos in play on branches, swinging,
chatting, laughing, I survey with skeptical eyes,
wishing to see a storybook with each trunk extension,
a bloodline of settlers who left safety behind,
wagons circled, fires lit, banjos strumming.

Or my childhood main street displayed
on a single branch: the undertaker, the small café,
the modest library where I read about pirates, pilots,
pioneers, dreaming of escaping this small town.

My tree now a concert hall, strains of a
Chopin nocturne rustle the leaves,
my hands entwined in twigs, my piano
silencing birds, delighting in trills.

I long to read this storybook, leave my porch,
become a child again, lie beneath that tree,
survey the soaring branches slivering the moon
against the darkening sky. Can I trust these aging bones
to find their way across the rutted ground,
climb over the wall, up the hill?

Queen Maple and I assess the risks.
Traces of lavender trail the setting sun,
the spirit calls the body to rest. Queen Maple
seeds the dreams of night. Surrender
to your imagination, for the soul never grows old.

Yes, I saw them, I tell my neighbor.
Did you hear them?

Fleeting Windows

My doctor says I'm losing my memory,
my friend confides as we drink
Ancient Happiness tea on her deck.
Clouds fold in deep fissures
like brain tissue over mountain peaks.
Do mountains have memory?

Feigning freshness, I recount again
how my son met his wife: an arranged
marriage in the Himalayan mountains,
Hindu rituals, henna hand painting,
my son's grand entrance to beating drums,
a bride in red and gold.

Our stories become fleeting windows
on an imagined train: our first dates
with husbands, my trip to Tunisia,
her love of skiing, B & B overnights
in Tudor homes, what to cook for supper.
Am I a travel companion, conductor, or guide?

Clouds smooth out, their folds flatten
over peaks, a layer of cream soothes
80 million-year-old rock. A shawl
of heather wraps the departing day.

The mountains tell us:
Live in the eternal now

The Botany of Grief

I.

You learn to love the place somebody leaves
behind for you.

~ Barbara Kingsolver

Take care of my plant, my stepson wrote
in careful script in his suicide letter
on the kitchen table of his apartment.
He placed the plant on a windowsill
to receive the afternoon sun.

This organized, reflective young man
folded and stacked t-shirts and socks,
made his bed daily, and earned A's
on college essays on his travel to India.

Did he pick this plant, knowing it was a croton?
I research its origins, its requirements,
a diversion from the awful truth:
Tim valued this plant more than life itself.

I search out a burnished ceramic crock,
fill it with rich potting soil, and plant
the croton in a sunny spot in our family room.
Soon vibrant red and yellow veins,
the kind crotons love to display,
emerge on its large shiny leaves.

The croton dislikes to be moved, I learn,
often dropping its leaves in trauma.

II.

The plants seemed to want me to share with the world
my own understanding of their beingness.

~ Jane Goodall

The honeymoon ended abruptly.
My flowered straw hat,
our Savannah pictures,
the recipes for Hoppin' John—
we had no time to unpack them
before the fateful telephone message.
I've run away from home and I won't tell you
where I am unless I can come live with you,
Tim cried into the phone to his dad.
I don't like to start a relationship
with a threat, Jeff said to me.
But where will he go? I anguished.
Tim came to live with us that night.

In our fledgling marital life, we had yet
to sort out who cooks dinner or
balances the checkbook, but we faced
a teenage boy out to flail against boundaries.
Punched holes in walls, drugs, slammed doors,
epithets, dirty underwear left to provoke
—and it did—ended my naive hope mothering
would ease his distress and settle him.
The great bindweed with its trumpet flowers
twists around other plants, takes over gardens,
chokes off life. Tim was my bindweed, difficult
to remove. And was that the solution?
Diagnosed with lobular breast cancer,
malignant threads that wove through tissue,
I uprooted him from our home.
Grief folded in on itself, dreams
of mothering, health, life itself, lost.

III.

...And here am I, budding
Among the ruins
With only sorrow to bite on,
As if weeping were a seed and I
The earth's only furrow.

~ Pablo Neruda

Tim returned when we moved to a prairie,
a farmhouse, barn and cottage. Native seeds,
buried for generations, emerged
as we burned off corn fields.

He lived in the cottage near our house,
close enough to cook with us each night
the chicken parmesan pasta dishes he loved
and wash the dishes, but far enough apart,
a peaceful resolution.

Like the big bluestem, larkspur and coneflowers,
he claimed roots in the soil and bloomed,
sharing his essays for an associate college degree
and organizing our recycling each week.

He loved the picture I captured of him cooking,
his face lit with a flash of smile. *Use it*
for my obituary, he said, an ominous quip.

None of his treatments worked.
Disease entangled Tim's brain.
This is not me! he lamented,
often after an outburst of anger.
We agreed, not the Tim we knew or loved.

IV.

Against this cosmic background the lifespan of a particular plant or animal appears, not as drama complete in itself, but only as a brief interlude in a panorama of endless change.

~ Rachel Carson

Tim's gone, leaving behind his croton.
I care for it, providing water, food,
and a prop to support its growing height.

A sturdy new branch adds dimension
to its upright stature, leaves reaching
for the sun and filling the window.

I know that it, like me, will not live forever.
But for today, I revel in its beauty.

Water pitcher in hand, I reach for it,
pausing to gaze at a nearby picture of Tim
in his rich brown embroidered Kurta,
dancing at his brother's India wedding,
arms raised, smiling gloriously.

The Moment

The moment dropped me into holiness:
flowered dresses, the pillow softness
of Kolaches, family stories of travel
across oceans, life during wartime,
and childhood games of hopscotch.

My grandmother's gilded teacup
and her shawl that wrapped my shoulders
brought past and present together.

It happened when no one was around:
Two years old, Raadhya climbed into my lap,
put her arm around my shoulder, and whispered
into my ear for the very first time
the dearest of words, *Grandma*.

My Life as a Mermaid

No child ever ponders, I didn't,
the practical consequences
of having a tail, not legs.

No one imagines a mermaid
at an outdoor art fair, a concert
in the park or at a mall shopping
for a prom dress with girlfriends.

Yet as I age, I find mermaid status
not so far-fetched for me. My feet
numb from neuropathy, I swerve
rather than walk down hallways,
touching walls for balance,
a fish maneuvering through
a fluid landscape.

In the pool, the water holds my body
in delicious suspension. Freed
to fling my arms, cycle my legs,
flip on my back, jog like a runner,
I imagine myself a dolphin,
whole here, an escapee
from graceless gravity.

Wildness

And the Blind One Shall Lead Us

The girl without sight
hears the rustle-grass
—an ant climbs the blade,
delighting in the view
of the dandelion at the mount.
We all say *Amen.*

The student without legs
rolls his wheelchair over dirt paths
to show us ancient Indian burial grounds,
pausing for tired feet, achy hips,
weak knees. Children witness his feat
and dream of a limitless future.

The girl on the spectrum, free
from distraction, focuses on survival
of the polar bear, the tiger, the fading
coral, clean air and water,
on scientists' alarm.

Unburdened by sound, the person
who is deaf casts the eye's golden light
on the agates, the ripple of stream,
the periwinkle early morning sky.

City of Women

Children eat breakfast every day at home
under the watch of someone who loves them,
the daycare worker basks in praise for nurturing
toddlers with adventure books as well as snacks,
the longtime maintenance worker sits with the CEO,
drinking coffee at an old oak table, talking
about her vision for the company's future.

Boundaries flux to welcome new refugees
searching for peace, away from violence,
away from rootlessness. Children teach adults
Hindi, Spanish, Swahili. Residents and newcomers
chat over chai, smiling and exchanging rituals
marking weddings and births, familiar and strange.

In this city of women, the bus driver creates
new routes to serve the stranded, the gardener
uses city funds to plant seas of red and purple
petunias in neglected neighborhoods,
the garbage collector plans the recycling plant.

Writers and artists bring together political partisans
to picnic in the city park and envision justice
for the aggrieved, freedom for the teen, now old.

Neighbors convert parking lots to vegetables gardens,
install merry-go-rounds, resurrect prairie grass
on land once belonging to native tribes.

Descendants of Sauk and Fox talk of land
billowing with wildrye, barley, foxtail and turkey foot.
Children giggle in their classroom and move closer.

Dancers approach strangers in the city square
to tango, rumba, waltz, to twirl orange and
red skirts, to shed jackets and ties,
restoring the childlike vigor of bodies
folded too long in chairs.

Living room lights set the city aglow.
Elders tell of adventurers seeking treasures,
only to return to the precious jewels of home.

The Muse

Her name was Emanuella
and she lived in Argentina.
By night she frequented milongas,
favoring the music of Piazolla
and the sad, velvet swoon
of the bandoneon.

She invited men to dance
with a swish of her black silk skirt,
slit to the thigh, and the flash of
the gold cross at the décolletage
of her scarlet satin blouse.

Don't hold back, she whispered
to fortunate partners, moving closer.
She barely noticed the applause
but loved it just the same.

Free to engage the world,
her spirit teases bodies who seek drama,
but shelter in safety. I know.
She visits my dreams, dismissing
my black pants and tunics,
cropped hair and rubber-soled shoes,
anathema to dance.

She adorns me with disorderly locks
and clothes that breathe freedom.
I become the dancer I desire,
turning halting steps into sultry sauntering
in piazzas of sunlit dance clubs
where revelers imbibe rum and romance.

By day, she delights in disruption.
She's back. It's the tango this time,
I whisper to my husband.

As my feet step, step, step, step, slide,
I smooth my rustling black skirt
and unbutton my blouse to breathe.

This Tree

Electric flash, rolling thunder jerk me,
coiled in blankets, from bed, out
toward the once quiet porch.

Lights out, I stumble, cling to
a flashlight leading to drama,
life reshaped, revealed in sharpness.

A giant Sawtooth Oak, tranquil by day,
a sanctuary for birds ejected now,
slashes the sky with ragged edges,
opening the divide: what is, what might be.

The charge: *Be a force*
for nature, for eyes that see,
for the beauty of this tree.

Blue Monkey Face

The blue monkey face with tall rust head feathers,
piercing red eyes, oversized blue ears, leers at me.

Embedded in my office Tunisian rug, he's surrounded
by crawling vines, wayward orange flowers, urns
the size of mountains, amoeba-shaped flourishes.

Though I've seen him many times, today
those eyes halt me with a question.

We met, that monkey face and I, on a forbidden trip
to the Medina, the old market of Tunis, the place
I was told not to go on my own. But a sunny day
and a waiting cab took me there anyway.

I was not long alone, for a man approached,
asking if he could help this young miss.
I want to buy a rug, I said.

More than eager, he waved, follow me. We wound up
ancient steps to view rooftop domes of gold and
chiseled stone, narrow winding streets, to hear
the swinging bells of mosques calling men
to leave their homes to pray.

More intrigued than afraid, I followed him
to arrive at a shop shrouded in rugs.
Young men dressed in sashed silk Jebbas
streamed from back rooms, carrying trays
of chai. Kneeling at my feet, they asked,
What does Madam want?

Prompted by my wishes, they rolled out
carpets of turquoise, red and rust, heavy
with ornament, inscribed with stories
of battles and feasts, ritual and debauchery.
The blue monkey face caught me.

With a stern stare and lips that formed *Oh*,
he appeared both disapproving and shocked.
I chose him, or did he choose me?

A credit card charge, a cab ride and
I was back at the home of my Tunisian hosts.
Aghast and angry, they admonished me,
You'll never see that rug, your card is stolen.

Weeks later my purchase arrived at the small
Iowa post office. *You look like a lady who would
order a rug from Tunis,* the postmaster said.

I've quit my corporate job, danced the Rumba,
performed Ragtime piano, frolicked with children,
cooked with Harissa, lived in the prairie, married for love.
In my seventies, what else is mine to do?

Claim your wildness, the Blue Monkey Face says.

Traveling Light

You've lost your fingerprints.
What have you done?

The Pre-Check TSA agent,
my ticket to stress-free travel,
quizzes me in a small Des Moines office
lodged between Thai and Mexican restaurants,
Tum Yum soup and enchiladas,
the Far East and Southern Hemisphere.

She waits for my answer.

I play the piano, I offer.
Fingerprints wear off when you play
Ragtime or Bach, clean, quick strokes,
all that precise pounding
people love but fingerprints don't.

Or maybe fingerprints, like eyebrows,
fall off as you get older. You aren't
the person you were.

Without Pre-Check, I take off
my shoes at Airport Security,
remove my computer from its case,
wait in long lines. My husband,
fingerprints intact, leaves ahead of me.

Polished, buffed, worn smooth
with time, I wear only the curious
self, stripped of worries, duties,
and now fingerprints.

Peering at paltry prints, dutifully,
rereading requirements, the agent
at last approves my application,
verification of who I am:

A woman who travels light.

The Grace of Aging

What I find humorous changes with age,
thanks to grandchildren who giggle
at the stories I dredge up from my past.

The time I jumped out of a slow-moving taxi
because the driver, stoned, traversed the lawn
of the Pentagon on the way to the airport.

Or when I went to a wedding reception,
discovering only when the bride appeared,
I was at the wrong event.

Or when I dropped my billfold into the toilet
and they found me drying my credit cards.
They agreed the billfold was odious,
their new word for the day.

Finding humor in silliness and humility
helps when makeup no longer covers wrinkles
and when parents yell at their children
Look out! as I approach with my cane.

Falling and rogue taxis can be dangerous,
but so is reluctance to share your stories,
which, untold, lodge in your heart
like brittle pieces of Christmas candy.

Lover of Life

I'm Nobody. Who are you?
Are you—Nobody—too?
                ~ Emily Dickinson

I'm nobody, devoid of titles,
of meetings in paneled boardrooms,
of endorsements once dearly sought.

No one applauds my early morning rituals:
drinking coffee with cream on a screened-in porch
or reading exotic South American novels
with screaming tropical birds, unsolved murders,
and illicit love affairs.

Few understand the thrill of faltering
fingers on piano keys, giving life to seven pages
of "Bachianas Brasileiras No. 5."

A four-year-old granddaughter learns to play jacks,
but her seven-year-old brother steals the ball
until she screams. When we settle back to play,
no one witnesses or approves.

None of the world's rewards compete
with the crunch of gravel on a sunset walk,
frogs croaking in the ditch,
my sweetheart's hand in mine.

I give up titles others bestow for this one: lover of life.

Unicorn Ears

The early morning sun
peeked into our kitchen.
What are you doing?
I asked my husband.

I am making unicorn ears,
he said, cutting yellow fondant
into diamonds, then pinching
and coaxing the sugary shapes
onto the frosted unicorn cake
our six-year old granddaughter
has requested for her birthday.

Why balance checkbooks
and clean bathrooms
when you can light
up a child's eyes?

What I Want to Remember

All good things are wild and free.
~ Henry David Thoreau

The Harvest Moon rises over
the farmhouse prairie, lighting the tips
of swaying big bluestem grass mango.
Dragonfly droves soar and dive,
kites liberated from string.
Grasshoppers spring their delight,
scattering us in surprise.

I fight for the survival of these
endangered memories, driving
through asphalt suburban streets,
once home to Echinacea, primrose,
wood lilies, and meadowlarks
building nests for their young.

A bulldozer tears up farmland
for concrete, burying dormant
prairie seeds in coffins,
their time to emerge forever gone.

Youth march and chant:
Save the earth for us and our children.
We're fighting for our future!
There is no Plan B.

They speak for my grandchildren,
too young to march, who play
in well-manicured city parks, unaware
the prairie once opened its arms
to children, including me.

Monarchs, the Red Admiral, and
the Blue Adonis blinked invitations
to hide and seek in seas of sunflowers.
The moon lights up switchgrass

and casts an amber glow
over milkweed and bergamot,
where once the Sauk and Fox roamed
with buffalo, elk, and coyote, free.
The wind remembers their stories.

Once I lived in a prairie farmhouse,
and I reside there still in my imagination.

Remembering Goat Haunt at Glacier National Park

We'd spent two weeks together
at the Qigong workshop, breathing in
chi from towering evergreens, imitating
grizzly bears and lions, wailing in the early
morning hours at the edge of water,
all on a quest to chase away our cancer.

After throwing their arsenal at me,
my western doctors gave me a 50/50
chance of surviving breast cancer.
Two Chinese doctors believed
in the power of Qigong.

Under a dome of blue skies, my new friends
and I hiked a gradual upward slope
of soft evergreen needles.
Geese flew overhead, knitting treetops.
Woodpeckers punctuated our steps.
Meadowlarks sang in grassy meadows.

The unexpected brought me to a halt:
a bridge made of wood slats and rope over
a vast canyon known as Goat Haunt.
Rushing water, melt from Glaciers,
surged below us. The bridge swayed.
Everyone but me scampered across.

From opposite sides of the canyon,
I felt the pull of their faith
in ancient traditions, my ability to
expel malignancy, now fear.

The friend I shared night-time stories with
waved. A serene Dr. Sha gazed at me.
Another guy made me laugh
with his best chimpanzee imitation.

Something, someone dissipated my fear.
My claws sank into the narrow slats.
My paws grasped the rope.
I walked across.

The Land Will Talk To You If You Listen

I walk without aim
across desert shrub grass.
Dust from blue gramma
sifts over my Adidas.
A sagebrush lizard leaps
into my wandering path.

I see pinon trees, sagebrush,
tumbleweed, the Rio Grande
now dry from drought,
what Tamayan Indian tribes
saw in settling here.

The land will talk to you if you listen.

Near the river, a toppled tree trunk
with two branches, a chest and arms,
an ancient fragment of a Roman bust.

Ants, aphids and beetles devour the soft,
spongy fibers, returning them to the earth.
Did this tree witness ancestral rituals
of Tamayan people?

The land will talk to you if you listen.

I meander alongside the river until
the late afternoon sun and an upsweep
of wind call me back.

But first, I turn to the ground
I've covered, startled to sense a shift—
a whiff of smoke, a flash of red,
a rattle punctuating the air.

Small rainbows bounce off bark
in the sun. The decaying trunk
transformed, arms now legs,
dances for me.

A rustle of sound, footsteps
on brush: the sun dips
below the horizon.

Acknowledgments

Later in life, I have discovered the joys of writing poetry, thanks to friends in the Transformational Language Arts Network. Three years ago, eleven of us participated in Right Livelihood Professional Training offered by TLA, a program designed to help you do what you love.

Led by Caryn Mirriam-Goldberg and Laura Packer, this program challenged me to share whatever wisdom I have to offer. The surprise was that sharing meant writing poetry.

Caryn, who became my poetry coach, taught me the fundamentals: line breaks, imagery, form, impact. Her wise and generous tending of my work became the seeds of *The Heart Hungers for Wildness*. The former Poet Laureate of Kansas, she models what she teaches, producing volumes of beautiful prose, fiction and poetry. Thank you, Caryn.

TLA friends Rachel Gabriel and Liz Burke-Cravens kept me going. We meet monthly to swap our poems, providing accountability for our craft. Local friend Pat Boddy and I meet bi-monthly with the same goal. Thanks to these three valuable poetry pals.

Mary Nilsen published the book through her company Zion Publishing. Her sense of style, elegant and engaging, shows in the selection of cover art, typeface, and organization. Thanks to Mary for walking me through the publishing process, as she did for my memoir, *This Need to Dance*.

Friends Mary Gottschalk and Carol Bodensteiner cast a careful eye on the manuscript to catch the errors in the next-to-final draft. Mary, Carol and I share a writing history. We worked together in developing our memoirs.

My family provided inspiration. Sisters Eileen Gamm, Sue Avila and I shared a peaceful small-town upbringing, thanks to our parents John and Helen Cox. My poems reflect that peaceful setting. Children Aaron Means and Saras Bhadri Means and grandchildren Soma and Raadhya added joy and humor. Tim, through his absence, is present in his own way.

My husband Jeff Means was more than a discerning reader. He suggested ideas for poems that resulted in "Blue Monkey Face," "Unicorn Ears," and "Curiosity." When my confidence flagged, as it does inevitably for writers, he cheered me on. He also appears in numerous poems, a sign of our close relationship. Thanks, Jeff, for believing in me and for your continuing enthusiasm.

I am living a good life (and a reasonably long one). Thanks to everyone who has played a part in getting me this far.

About the Author

Diane Glass brings a writer's astute attention to detail and a spiritual director's probing of depth to bring new meaning to everyday experience in her new book of poetry, *The Heart Hungers for Wildness.*

You may resonate with specific life situations—the grief of losing a child, the joy of becoming a grandmother, the difficulty of dealing with illness, or the adventure of exploring the natural world. Most certainly you will identify with the universal themes of change, loss, renewal, and gratitude that arise from her poems.

Diane's powerful memoir, *This Need to Dance,* broke new ground in revealing her life with spina bifida. Her work has been published in the "Des Moines Register," "The Iowan," "Dragonfly Arts Magazine," and as essays in various publications.

After a career as a Des Moines Register executive, she served as a spiritual director and teacher at the Des Moines Pastoral Counseling Center. She and her husband Jeff Means and their cat Penelope live in Des Moines

Made in the USA
Coppell, TX
17 January 2021

48336085R00046